Guinea Pigs

How to
tr

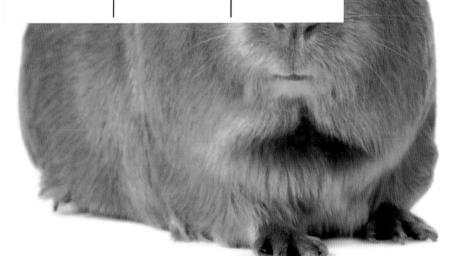

Heather Maisner

OXFORD
UNIVERSITY PRESS

OXFORD
UNIVERSITY PRESS

Great Clarendon Street, Oxford OX2 6DP

Oxford University Press is a department of the University of Oxford.
It furthers the University's objective of excellence in research, scholarship,
and education by publishing worldwide in

Oxford   New York

Auckland   Cape Town   Dar es Salaam   Hong Kong   Karachi
Kuala Lumpur   Madrid   Melbourne   Mexico City   Nairobi
New Delhi   Shanghai   Taipei   Toronto

With offices in

Argentina   Austria   Brazil   Chile   Czech Republic   France   Greece
Guatemala   Hungary   Italy   Japan   Poland   Portugal   Singapore
South Korea   Switzerland   Thailand   Turkey   Ukraine   Vietnam

Oxford is a registered trade mark of Oxford University Press
in the UK and in certain other countries

British Library Cataloguing in Publication Data

Data available

ISBN-13: 978-0-19-911580-8

1 3 5 7 9 10 8 6 4 2

Printed in Singapore by Imago

MEET TOFFEE

Name:	Toffee Smith
Age:	6 months
Breed:	Short-haired
Lives:	Swansea, Wales
Owner:	Rosie Smith, aged 6

I am writing this for Rosie and her friends,
so that they understand me and we can all live happily together.

Toffee

Look at me!

I'm gentle and friendly. I never bite or scratch.
I love being with people and I think I make the best pet of all.

Guinea pigs belong to a big group of animals
called rodents. Other rodents are hamsters,
gerbils, mice, rats and chinchillas.
Rodent means 'to gnaw' and
all rodents have two teeth
at the top and two at
the bottom of the jaw
that keep on growing.
So we have to
gnaw constantly.

My **hair** covers my whole body,
except my ears.

My **nose** is soft and very sensitive.

My **mouth** is big and I have twenty teeth.

My **whiskers** are sensitive, too.
I use them to feel my way through holes.

My **eyes** are bright and round, and hardly ever close or blink. They are at the side of my head so I can see enemies above, behind me and in front of me.

My **eyebrows** are long and sensitive, like a cat's whiskers.

My **ears** are large and drooping with a bald patch behind. I can hear the faintest sound.

My front legs have four **tiny toes** with sharp claws. I use these to hold down food.

My **short front legs** are close together. My two back legs are wider apart and larger.

My **strong back legs** have three toes with big thick claws. I use them to push up and run when I'm scared.

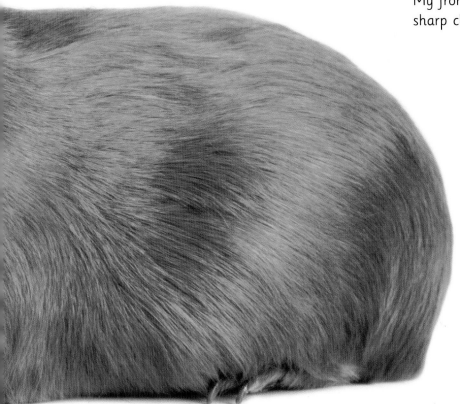

My **belly** is large and plump for digesting plant food.

Different breeds

A guinea pig is a kind of rodent called a cavy. The people who first saw a guinea pig thought its short legs and plump body were like a pig's. They also thought it came from Guinea in Africa, so they called it a guinea pig.

There are over 30 different kinds, or breeds, of guinea pig and lots of cross breeds. The main breeds are recognised by their coats. Guinea pigs that are all one colour are called selfs. Non-selfs can have up to three colours in their coats.

My friend Bertie is an **Abyssinian** with rough hair that grows in a pattern of rosettes.

Pinky and Perky are **Peruvians.** They have silky hair right down to the ground and long fringes that have to be brushed away from their eyes.

Bill and Ben are **Agoutis**. The tips of their hair are lighter than the roots which makes them look speckled.

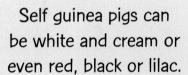

Self guinea pigs can be white and cream or even red, black or lilac.

I'm a **self** guinea pig. My coat is all one reddish colour. I think it looks very smart.

My family

Guinea pigs come from
South America, where they
live in groups in the
mountains and grasslands.
They are most active at dawn
and dusk when it is harder
for them to be spotted by
animals who hunt them.
Local people used to
breed them for food.

My cousin the **Chinchilla**
lives in the Andes Mountains.
She has soft grey fur and
leaps from rock to rock.

Maras are also known as **Patagonian Cavies**. They live in small groups in Argentina and some other parts of South America. Here are some babies.

Maras run very fast and can leap up to six feet in the air! They run about in the day and burrow underground at night.

My cousin the **Rock Cavy** loves climbing and jumping, and lives in trees and rocks.

Birth and early life

Female guinea pigs are called sows, males are boars and the babies are pups.

A sow can have babies when she is five weeks old.
She usually gives birth to about three babies. My mum had four.

At five weeks, boys and girls must be separated
or they may start having families of their own.

I was born with two brothers and a sister. As soon as I was born, my mum **licked me clean**.

I was born with all my **fur**. My **eyes** were open and I had all my **teeth**.

I **suckled** my mother for about three weeks. After a few days, I could eat solid food, too.

Pups love being with their brothers and sisters. They **purr** to each other all the time.

At the end of one week, I could **walk** quite fast. At five weeks, I was old enough to leave my mother and go to a new home.

Choosing our owners

Guinea pigs like living together. It is best to buy at least two of the same sex from the same litter. If you buy a boy and a girl, they will have lots of babies.

Some of us need more looking after than others. Long-hairs need grooming every day. Be sure to pick the guinea pig that's right for you.

Pet shops usually have a good choice of guinea pigs and hamsters. Or you can go to a breeder. A young guinea pig is easier to tame than an older one.

I live with my sister in a **hutch** outside in the **garden**. Our friend Floppy lives **indoors** with his brother in a **run** with a **covered top**. His owner, Maya, looks after them well.

Do not choose a pet because you feel sorry for it. If it has bald patches, sneezes and wheezes, is hunched up and sleepy, it is probably ill.

Rosie chose me. I'm alert and healthy. My coat is **sleek** and I scamper all over the place. I have **short hair** so I'm easy to look after.

Floppy has **long hair**.
He needs grooming every day.

Learning through play

At first, when I arrived home, I was very nervous. Rosie sat quietly beside me. She talked to me and offered me a carrot stick. I sniffed and nibbled it.

Rosie **strokes** me very **gently**. She talks quietly and never shouts. And she never, ever squeezes me.

Now, I know Rosie's voice and I **chirrup** and call when I hear her.

After a day or two, you can kneel down and **pick me up** very carefully. Put one hand under my chest and the other under my bottom.

If I **struggle** because I feel uncomfortable, slowly put me down on the ground.

Never drop your guinea pig. Carefully put her down or you could cause serious damage to her insides.

When I'm hungry

We're vegetarians and eat only plants and seeds. You can buy packets of dry food from the pet shop and give us fresh food, too.

We have two meals a day. We love broccoli, cauliflower, kale, lettuce, pepper, carrots, eating apples, pears and oranges.

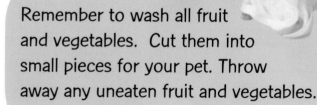

Remember to wash all fruit and vegetables. Cut them into small pieces for your pet. Throw away any uneaten fruit and vegetables.

Put out **dry food** in a solid, heavy bowl, so we can't knock it over.

Sometimes you can give us **bran mash** in another bowl. We also like wild **grasses**, **dandelion leaves** and **clover**.

If guinea pigs eat their own droppings, don't worry. This is natural. They need to eat their food twice.

We **drink water** from a special **bottle** with a drip feed. You can attach it to my cage. We push the ball back with our tongues to let the water out.

Attach the water bottle to the cage at a height your pet can easily reach. Give your pet **fresh water every day**.

Be careful not to give your pet any poisonous plants. Check with an adult first.

When I'm happy

I'm happy when I huddle together with my family and friends. I love it when we go exploring.

I'm happy when you **scratch** me behind the **ears**. If you **tickle** me under the **chin**, I'll lift my head higher and higher. I'll close my eyes and look very pleased.

We're always **happy** when we're sitting quietly in our owner's arms. We love being **gently stroked** and make lots of different sounds to show we're contented. Guinea pigs talk a lot: we **purr** when we're happy, **squeal** when we're hurt and **murmur** quietly when we're munching our way through dinner.

We all use our cheeks, backs and bottoms to **mark** things that belong to us with our **scent**. That could even be you!

We **sniff** the air to see if anyone is near. We sniff a friend's nose or bottom to double check he is our friend.

19

Keep away!

We are usually very peaceful but sometimes males, called boars, get into a fight.

When Boris had a **fight** with Ted, they both made **aggressive noises**. Boris's **teeth chattered**. Then he opened his mouth wide, like he was yawning, but really he was showing his very sharp teeth.

Boris and Ted **stood** on their **back legs** and rammed their heads together. Their mouths were wide open, ready to bite.

When two boars fight, throw a towel over them or ask an adult to separate them. Wear heavy gloves.

When we get **angry**, we make our **hair stand on end** so that we look bigger and more threatening. We also make our teeth chatter.

When we are **frightened**, we **freeze** to the spot. We think our enemies won't see us if we stand very still. If I throw my head back, when you stroke me, please stop at once. It means I'm not in the mood.

When I'm tired

We sleep for about 5 hours a day but hardly ever close our eyes. We're always on the lookout for danger and never sleep for more than 10 minutes at a time.

My outdoor hutch has a separate area for **sleeping**.

Rosie lined it with **wood shavings** and put in lots of hay for my bed and for me to hide in. I like to nibble the hay, too.

Gerald lives **indoors** in a **run** with a **covered top**. He doesn't have a separate area for sleeping.

If we run around the house or on the lawn, we may not be easy to catch. You can steer us into a cardboard box lined with hay.

Washing and grooming

Short-haired or rough-haired guinea pigs are easy to keep clean. Long-haired guinea pigs with hair down to the ground need brushing and combing every day.

Use fingers to untangle knots in your pet's fur. Brush fur away from the head. Brush the tummy and under the chin. Then use a comb.

Floppy likes it when Maya holds him in her arms each day and **brushes** him. **Hay** and **dirt** are always getting stuck in Floppy's **long coat**. He needs brushing at least once a day.

Use special shampoo from the pet shop and rub it in with your fingers. Always keep the face dry. Rinse well until all the bubbles disappear.

I **lick** myself **clean** with my tongue and use my front teeth and back claws like a comb.

Sometimes we like a good **wash**. Put **warm water** in a bowl, gently lower us in and wash us gently. Then **rub** us carefully with a **towel** until we are dry. Remember to **keep us warm**. Brrr! Lovely!

Keeping healthy

Every day, Rosie checks that my fur is soft and clean and that I don't have any wounds or infections. She looks at my back, my tummy and my legs. She checks that my eyes are bright and my ears are clean.

Lift up each foot to see if our claws have grown too long.

Check our teeth and gums for infections.

Once a week, Rosie weighs me. If I'm too heavy, it means I need more exercise. If I've lost weight, it may mean that I'm ill and need to see the vet.

Every day Rosie **washes** out my **food bowl** and fills my water bottle with **fresh water**. She changes my **bedding**, too.

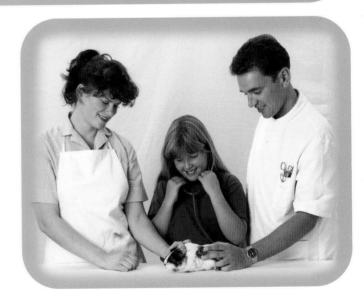

We should have a check up with the vet once a year.

Your pet and others

We are very small creatures, easily frightened, and we spend a lot of time protecting ourselves. We are frightened of other animals, especially cats. In the wild we are prey to big cats, like pumas.

Dogs are also big and frightening so please be careful when you introduce us. Be sure your dog is **gentle** and keep hold of his collar. He could get playful or aggressive and hurt us.

Sometimes we like living with other animals of similar size, like **rabbits**. We get on really well together

I'm very **happy** living with other guinea pigs.

Goodbye!

I've loved writing this book;
I hope it's helped you understand
what makes me happy!

Toffee

FIND OUT MORE

Some useful websites:

www.pdsa.org.uk

www.bbc.co.uk/cbbc/wild/pets

www.allaboutpets.org.uk

All images © DK images, except the following:
© Corbis: 9t + bl
© Getty: 21c
© Alamy: 29cr

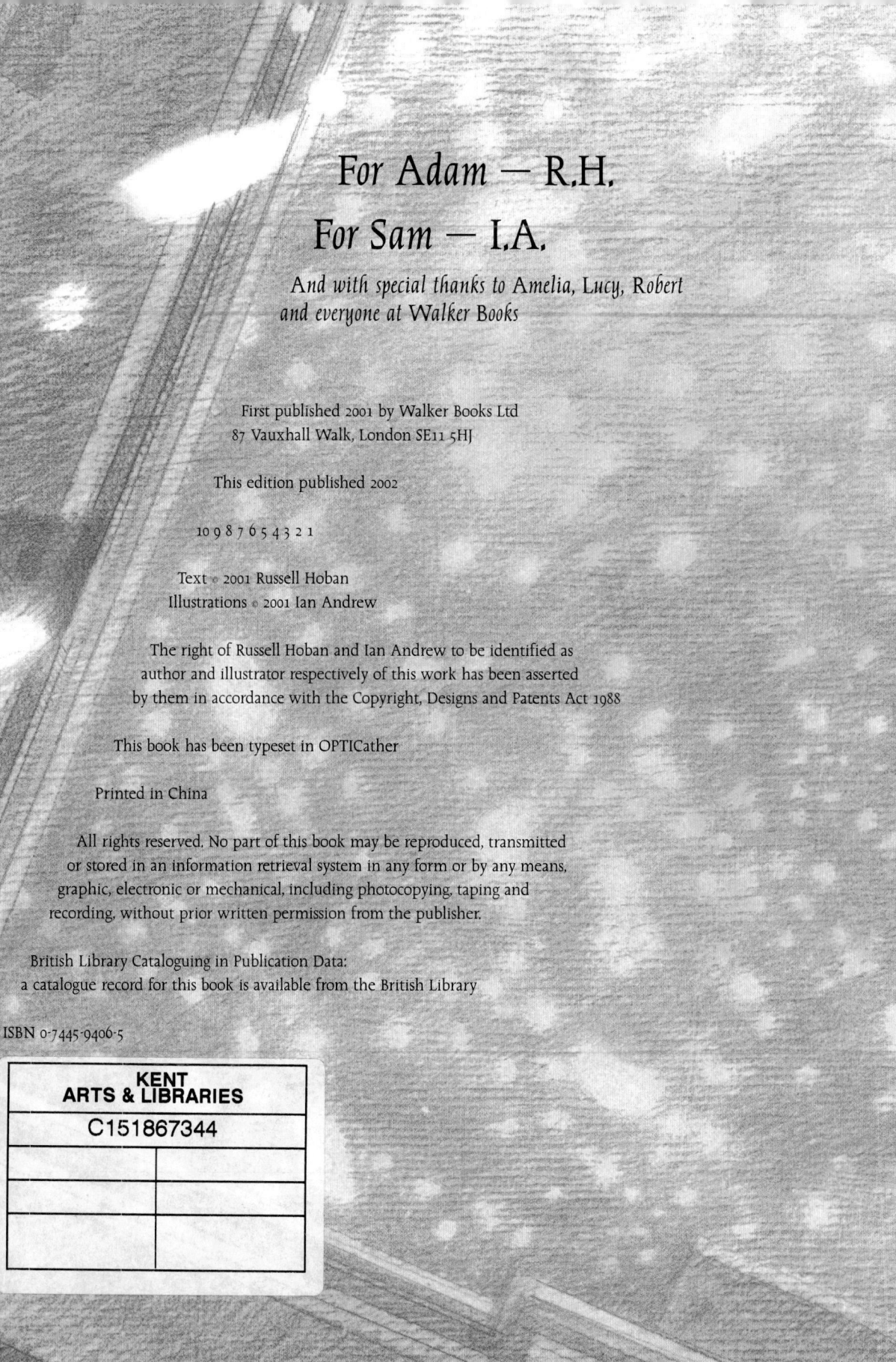

For Adam — R.H.
For Sam — I.A.

*And with special thanks to Amelia, Lucy, Robert
and everyone at Walker Books*

First published 2001 by Walker Books Ltd
87 Vauxhall Walk, London SE11 5HJ

This edition published 2002

10 9 8 7 6 5 4 3 2 1

Text © 2001 Russell Hoban
Illustrations © 2001 Ian Andrew

The right of Russell Hoban and Ian Andrew to be identified as
author and illustrator respectively of this work has been asserted
by them in accordance with the Copyright, Designs and Patents Act 1988

This book has been typeset in OPTICather

Printed in China

British Library Cataloguing in Publication Data:
a catalogue record for this book is available from the British Library

ISBN 0-7445-9406-5

JIM'S LION

WRITTEN BY
RUSSELL HOBAN

ILLUSTRATED BY
IAN ANDREW

WALKER BOOKS
AND SUBSIDIARIES
LONDON · BOSTON · SYDNEY

From his hospital bed Jim was watching the snow whirling out of the grey sky. He was looking sad. Nurse Bami brought him hot chocolate. She was from Africa; she had tribal scars on her cheeks. She had seen lions, elephants, crocodiles.

"What's the matter?" said Bami.

"You know," said Jim.

"Tell me," said Bami. "Say it out."

"People who have what I have, mostly they die, don't they?" said Jim.

"Maybe the doctors can fix you up," said Bami.

"I've seen what they do on TV," said Jim. "They put you on a table and they put you to sleep and then they do the rest of it."

"Does that scare you?" said Bami.

"Yes," said Jim. "When I'm asleep I go to different places in my dreams but I always find my way back. I'm afraid that if the doctors put me to sleep they might send me somewhere that I can't get back from."

"Well, of course someone has to come looking for you," said Bami.

"Who can do that?" said Jim.

"Drink your hot chocolate," said Bami, "and I'll tell you."

"When you think of something, you see it in your head, don't you?" said Bami.

"Sure I do," said Jim.

"Listen carefully now," said Bami. "This is not kid stuff."

"Good," said Jim.

"You've got all kinds of things in your head," said Bami, "everything you've ever seen or thought about, all in your head."

"I can't remember it all," said Jim.

"But it's all there," said Bami, "and there are all kinds of animals in there along with everything else."

"I guess there are," said Jim.

"One of those animals is the finder who can bring you back from wherever the doctors send you," said Bami.

"Which one?" said Jim.

"That's not for me to say," said Bami. "You must find your finder by yourself."

"How can I do that?" said Jim.

"That's what I'm going to tell you," said Bami.

"Close your eyes," said Bami, "and let
everything go away so your mind is empty."

Jim did that.

"Now," said Bami, "let a place come into your mind,
a place where you really felt good. Don't
tell me what it is, just let it come to you."

The place that came to Jim was a lonely place by the sea.
It was near an empty harbour that used to be full of
fishing boats. He'd been there with Mum and Dad
a long time ago, before his illness.

"When you see that place," said Bami, "let yourself
hear it and smell it and taste it and touch it."

Jim did that. He saw the sea and the long, long sky
in the summer afternoon. There was a great brown rock
that stuck out of the sea, it was called the Lion's Head.
Jim saw shags flying low over the water, he heard the
wind and the crying of the gulls. He heard the sighing of
the sea and the hissing of it on the sand. He heard the
pebbles clicking in the tide-wash.

Jim smelled the salt wind and the sea and the
sun-warm rocks on the beach. He put his hand
in the water, felt the deep coldness of it
and tasted the salt on his hand. He touched
the rocks and felt the long years in them.
He felt good in that place by the sea.

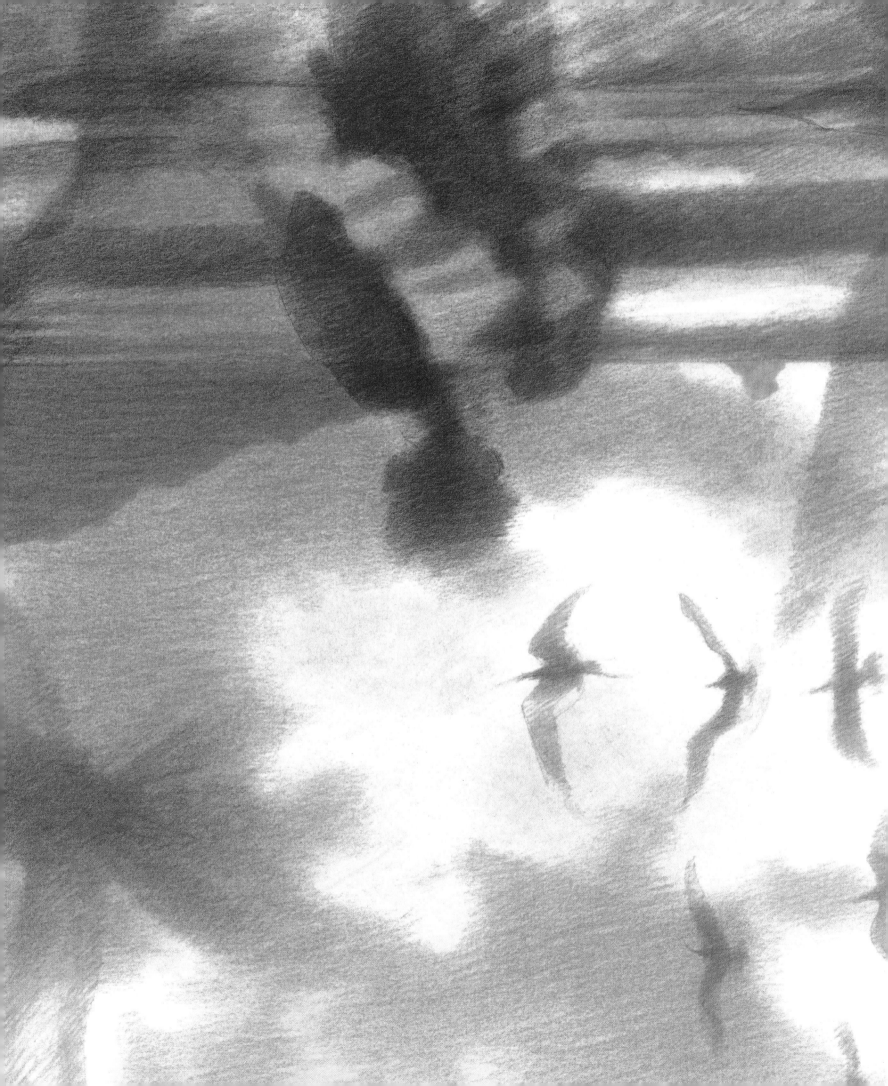

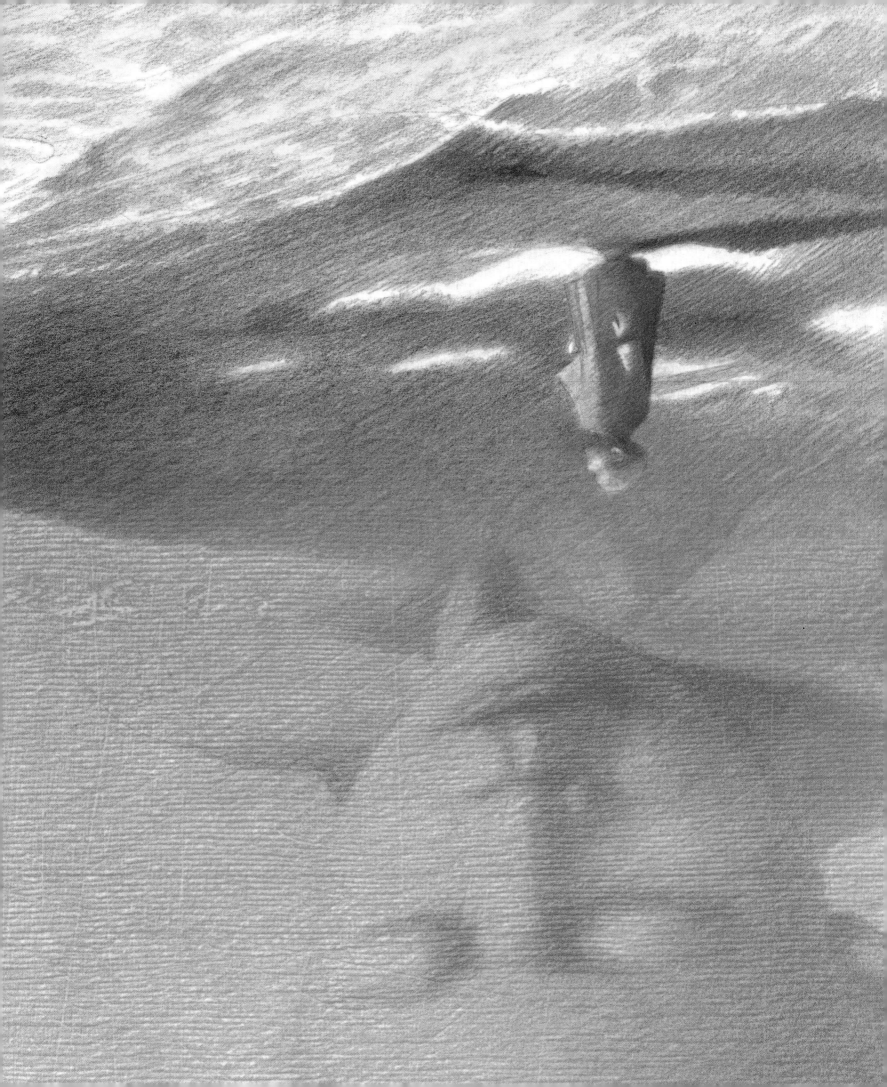

"Are you feeling good?" said Bami.
Jim didn't answer. He was smiling and he was asleep.
He was in that good place by the sea. He could feel
that he was waiting for the moon to rise.
When it came up he saw that it was a full moon.
The wet sand was all silvery with it. "Here I am," said Jim,
"waiting." Then he saw a small dark shape far down the beach.
Slowly it got bigger as it moved towards him. It was a lion.

"There aren't any
lions around here," said Jim.
He ran to the cliffs on the shore
and climbed to the top
and woke up.

"Good morning," said Bami. "Don't tell me your dream, keep it inside you. Here comes breakfast."

"Why can't I tell you my dream?" said Jim.

"If it happened in your good place it might be a finding dream," said Bami, "and if you talk about it something goes out of it."

"Have you got a finder?" said Jim.

"Oh yes," said Bami, "I'd have been dead three or four times already if my finder hadn't come looking for me."

"Is your finder an animal?" said Jim.

"Yes, but I won't say which one," said Bami.

"How did you find it?" said Jim.

"I went to my good place in a dream," said Bami, "and it came to me there."

"Did it, you know, scare you at all?" said Jim.

"Yes," said Bami. "That's how I knew it was the real thing. The real thing is always more than you're ready for. Of course I had my don't-run stone with me."

"A don't-run stone!" said Jim. "I haven't got one."

"Now you do," said Bami. She took a little painted pebble out of her pocket and gave it to Jim. "Don't ask me any more questions," she said. "You must go on alone from here."

Jim's mum and dad were talking to Jim's doctor, Dr Monjo.

"Will Jim get better?" said Mum.

"It depends," said Dr Monjo, "on what Jim has going for him."

"Don't you know?" said Mum. "Haven't you done all kinds of tests?"

"Yes," said Dr Monjo, "but the tests don't always tell us why some people get better and others don't."

"Isn't there an operation you can do?" said Dad.

"There is," said Dr Monjo, "but I'm not sure he's in good enough shape for it."

"When will you know?" said Dad.

"Let's see how he is in a day or two," said Dr Monjo.

Mum and Dad brought Jim grapes and clementines and his big animal book that he'd asked for.

"Are you eating properly?" said Mum. "You have to keep your strength up."

"Yes," said Jim, "I'm eating properly and I'm feeling stronger all the time."

"That's the ticket," said Dad.

"Maybe you'll be home for Christmas," said Mum.

"I'm working on it," said Jim.

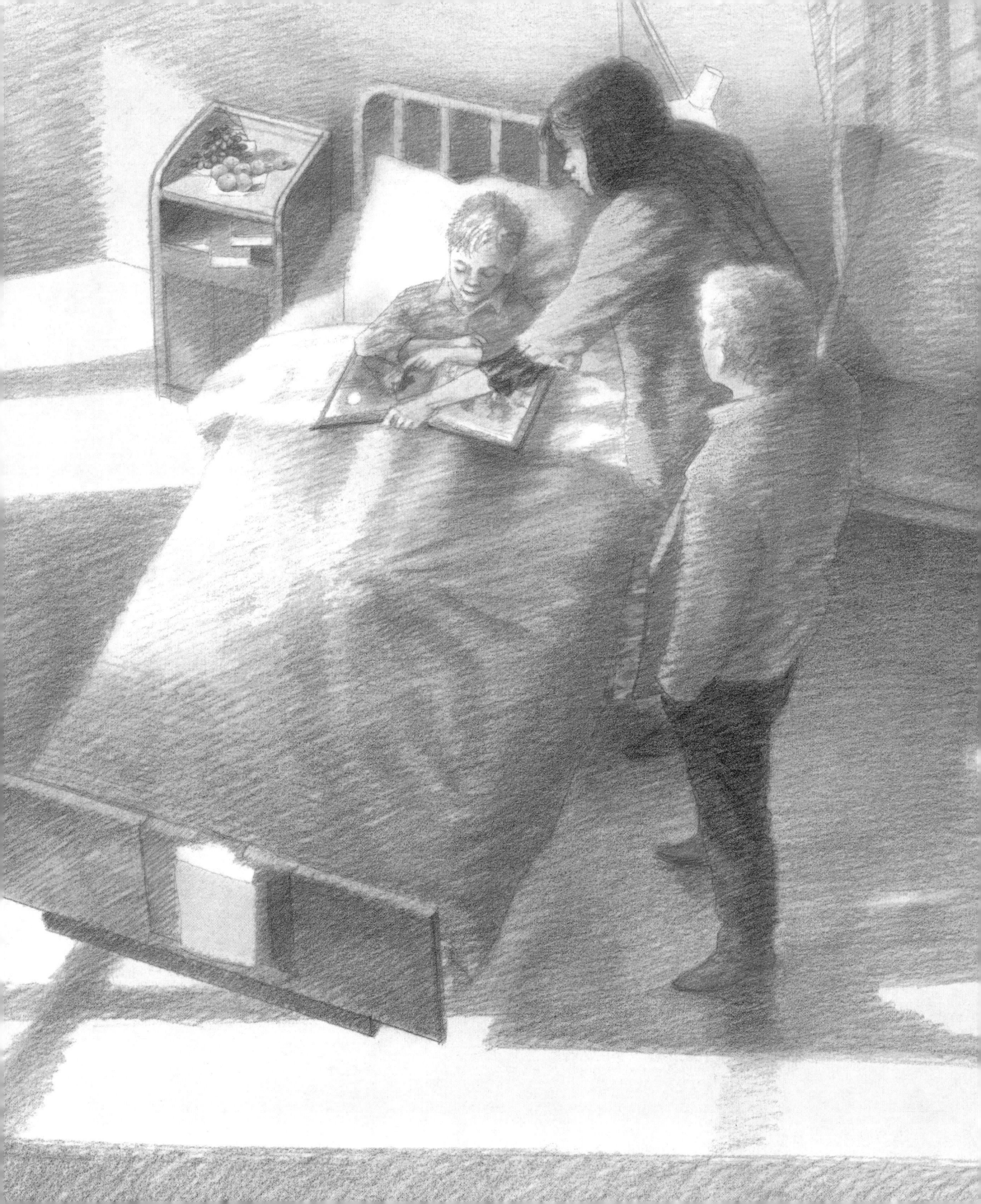

That night in his dream Jim was back at the place by the sea. The moon was still full and the lion was still coming towards him. Jim wanted to climb up the cliffs but he had the don't-run stone in his hand and he didn't. "The real thing is always more than you're ready for," he said.

Closer and closer came the lion.

"Maybe," said Jim, "everything else was a dream and this is the only thing that's real."

Closer and closer came the lion. It opened its mouth and roared.

"Maybe this lion will eat me up," said Jim, "and nobody will know that I didn't run."

Closer came the lion with its amber eyes, its pink tongue and white teeth.

"Are you my finder?" said Jim.

The lion roared again.

"Maybe that means yes," said Jim.

He stood where he was until
the lion was so close that he could
smell its hot breath.

"I'm going to touch you," said Jim,
"and if you're my finder you
won't eat me up."

He stretched out his hand
as the lion came closer. Now
the lion was right in front of
Jim and he put his hand on
its head and woke up.

"Well, Jim," said Dr Monjo, "the latest tests are looking pretty good and you're looking pretty good too."

"I feel good," said Jim. He was remembering how he'd put his hand on the lion's head.

"I'll have to talk to your mum and dad," said Dr Monjo, "but first I want to talk to you. There's an operation that could help you but there's always some danger and I want you to tell me how you feel about it. Do you want to do it?"

"Yes," said Jim, "let's do it."

"You sound very confident," said Dr Monjo.

"I know you're a good doctor," said Jim, "and the rest of it I'll leave to my finder."

"Who's your finder?" said Dr Monjo.

"I mustn't say," said Jim.

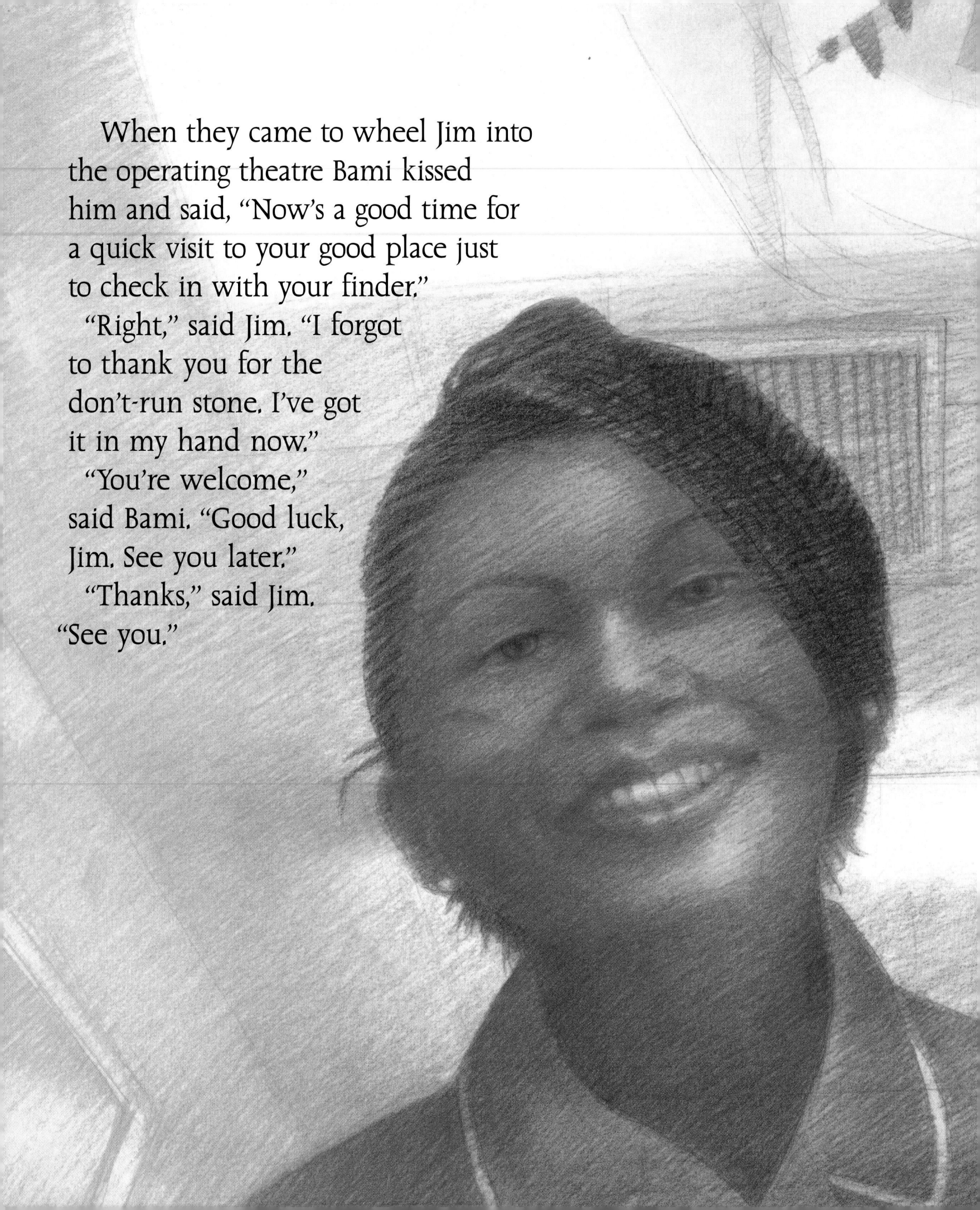

When they came to wheel Jim into
the operating theatre Bami kissed
him and said, "Now's a good time for
a quick visit to your good place just
to check in with your finder."

"Right," said Jim. "I forgot
to thank you for the
don't-run stone. I've got
it in my hand now."

"You're welcome,"
said Bami. "Good luck,
Jim. See you later."

"Thanks," said Jim.
"See you."

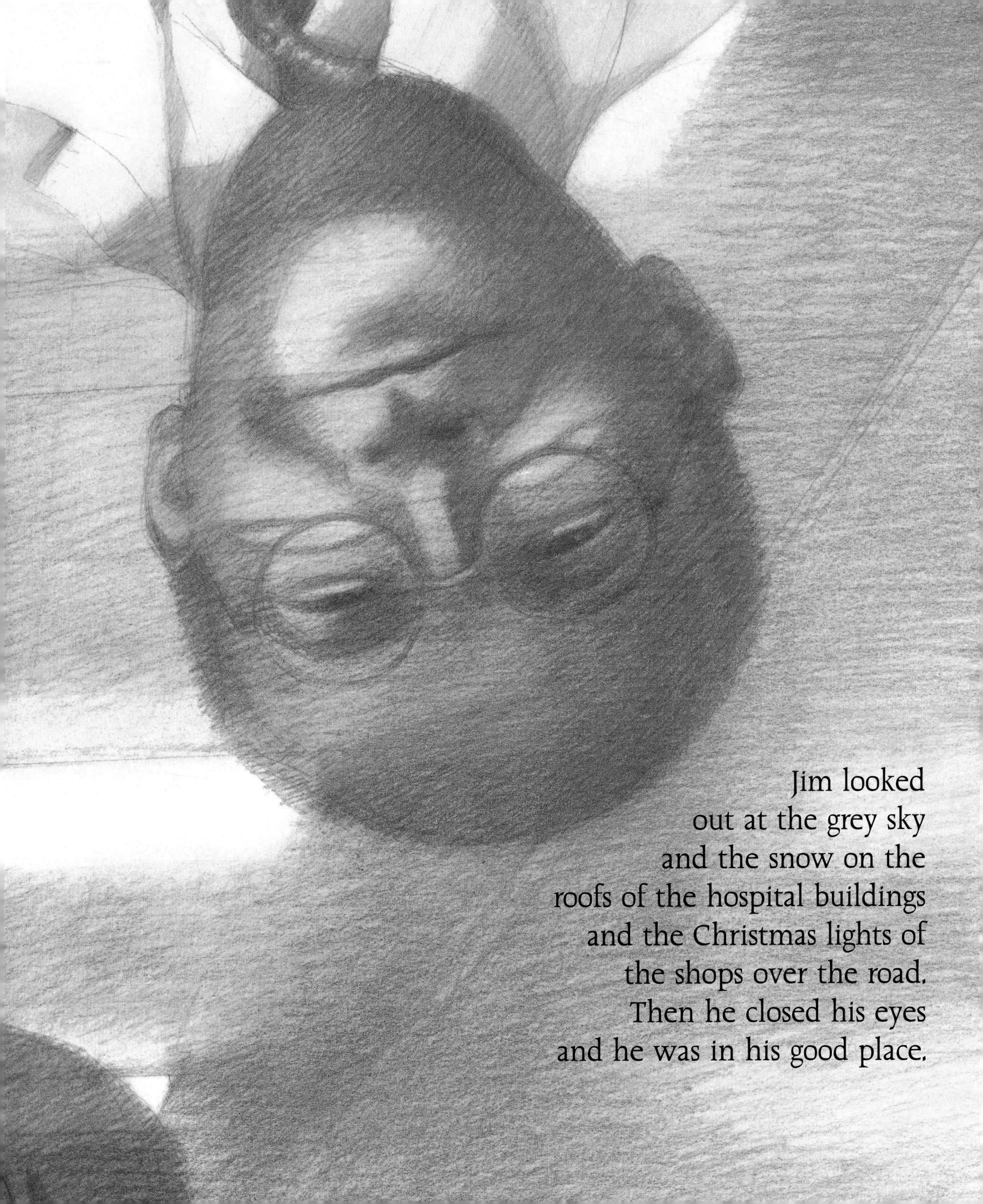

Jim looked
out at the grey sky
and the snow on the
roofs of the hospital buildings
and the Christmas lights of
the shops over the road.
Then he closed his eyes
and he was in his good place.

There was no moon but in the
starlight he could see the lion sitting
on the beach the way a dog sits.
It was waiting for him.

Jim looked into the lion's
amber eyes and the lion
opened its mouth and roared.

"OK," said Jim, "let's do it."
He walked down the long curve
of the beach into the dark
and the lion followed.

On Christmas morning Jim came downstairs in his pyjamas and looked at the Christmas tree with its fairy lights. He remembered how his lion looked coming through the dark to find him.

"Happy Christmas!" said Mum and Dad.

"Happy Christmas," said Jim. "I haven't had a chance to get your presents."

"You're our present," said Mum.

"The best that could ever be," said Dad.

Jim got a train set and a computer game from Mum and Dad. There was another box, a small one. Jim opened it and there was a beach pebble inside the wrappings.

On it was written:

This is to remember me by.
It is from my good place.

Love xx, Bami.

RUSSELL HOBAN says that the lion in *Jim's Lion*,
"is an old friend of mine. We've travelled far together
and he's always brought me back."

Russell was born in Pennsylvania, USA and was an illustrator
before he became a writer. He has more than sixty picture books
to his name, including *The Sea-thing Child*, illustrated by
Patrick Benson and shortlisted for the Kate Greenaway Medal.
He lives in London.

IAN ANDREW says of *Jim's Lion*, "The illustrations
of the special place that Jim goes to in his dreams are based
closely on a special place from my own childhood –
the Dingle Peninsula in Ireland."

Ian has worked on numerous animated films as well as illustrations
for children's books. Another title for Walker is *The Midnight Man*
by Berlie Doherty. Ian lives in Croydon, Surrey.